Wishing you
a successful Omni
Management Conference

Marc Reydolous

Washington September 25th 1985

PRESTIGE

CHAMPAGNE
AND
THE BELLE
ÉPOQUE

PERRIER-JOUËT/NATHAN INTERNATIONAL

An absolute triumph at the 1889 World Exhibition.

THE EIFFEL TOWER AND FRENCH NATIONAL PRIDE

It's the *Belle Epoque* and the Champagne flows, or so goes the song. In our mind's eye it's aglow with a thousand lights. It moves, it sways, it's alive. Pink or gold. The *Belle Epoque* was the golden era for Champagne according to the wine's historian, François Bonal. 1889: the curtain is about to go up on the 20th Century. We are entering the era of the consumer society. « The French are so rich, wrote Arthur Conte in his text "1er janvier 1900" (Ed. Plon), that their young Finance Minister dares dream of personal income tax. It's as though life were suddenly something light and gay. » The moderate republicans were at the helm of the ship of state sailing over calm waters.

The bronze group by Dalou illustrates the triumph of the republic and was a symbol of this joy in being French. It was erected on the Place de la Nation and was unveiled at the end of the 1889 World Exhibition, dawn of this *Belle Epoque* which was stepping out in an "allegro vivace" tempo. The Exhibition was inaugurated on May 6th by President Carnot and celebrated the centenary of the Republic which was sorely in need of reinforcing its foundations, its power and its legitimacy. All of these were under attack from nostalgic royalists, radical revisionists and the repeated assaults by General Boulanger, who was forced to leave the country. The September elections held in the afterglow of the Exhibition's success assured the régime that its roots had taken in the four corners of the land. The country had not yet been shaken by the Dreyfus affair. The anarchists were hatching obscure plots, the Panama scandal had not yet broken.

On the banks of the Seine, the Eiffel Tower stood proudly as an expression of French genius and an epoch which was "ugly, rich and happy" (Paul Morand, 1931).

The Exhibition, a maze of discoveries

The Eiffel Tower was named after Gustave Eiffel, the famous engineer who designed it and who was a specialist in metal construc-

tions. Some 15 000 pieces of metal 10 mm thick drilled with 7 million holes went into its construction. It took two years to build and cost 7 million francs in 1889. At the time of its construction it weighed 7 000 tons.

A fine restaurant, "Le Brébant", was installed on the first platform — which already said much for the Tower's future. There were also a Russian restaurant and an English one, as well as a Flemish bar. On the second platform, the newspaper "Le Figaro" opened an editorial office and set up a press to print a 4-page paper. On the third platform a telegraph office was opened where 8 employees and 4 postmen worked. The tower, the Machine Gallery and the Colonial Exhibition were the three highlights of the 1889 Exhibition which spread from the Trocadero Palace to the Champ de Mars far below Eiffel's metal girders.

Pavilions and divas

The Exhibition was perhaps just the glory hole of the period like the poem by Jacques Prévert, "Inventaire", written a few decades later, though with a little less of the poet's art. Here could be found everything that was France, at home and in the four corners of the globe. The visitor could see and hear the history of housing since the beginning of time, take a stroll by the Tobacco, Gas, or Fire Pavilions, stop wondrous before the Bohemian divas, the Fine Arts Pavilion (with Gallé), locomotives, the Kabyle women's tent in the Algerian Palace. It was a maze of modern discoveries and constructions all of which contributed to the enthusiastic pride in "maintaining and protecting the nation's unity".

Left: visiting the Exhibition, a trip to the Eiffel tower.
Right: Champagne bubbled everywhere.
An advertisement for a restaurant by Chéret.

"Nature unveiling before science" by Barrias in silver and vermeil.

Champagne was no stranger to the party. An enormous cask holding the equivalent of 200 000 bottles was deposited at the foot of the Tower having been drawn by 24 oxen all the way from Epernay and the Mercier cellars. To get this colossus there, it had been necessary to demolish a few houses and reinforce several bridges...

From 1889 to 1900 the country was to sink to abysmal depths. In 1894 President Carnot was assassinated by terrorists. The so-called "*scélérat*" or blackguard laws were passed to counter anarchists who were creating unrest. Scandals (Panama) and attacks were disrupting "French order and peace". Amidst all the fuss, the separation of the Church and the State was accomplished virtually unnoticed.

Dreyfus, a name not to be mentioned

At the end of 1894, Captain Dreyfus, an Alsatian Jew, was accused of treason. He was arrested and the "traitor" was stripped of his rank, and sentenced to deportation for life on Devil's Island. The press seized the opportunity and inflamed public opinion. France was divided: liberals against conservatives. In families Dreyfus' supporters were pitted against his opponents. Politicised rallies turned into witch hunts. The Republic itself was in danger.

A famous cartoon by Caran d'Ache entitled "A Family Dinner" was published in "Le Figaro" on 13 February 1898. Ten typical bourgeois are gathered around the table. As the servant brings in the soup tureen, the master of the house says: "Above all, don't talk about the Dreyfus affair". A little later on, table and chairs overturned, all the diners have come to blows. "They talked about it!"

The innocent Jew was brought back after ten years exile in the penal settlement following publication in "L'Aurore" of the famous open letter, "J'accuse...", by Emile Zola. But the wound had gone to the very heart of the country and took a long time to heal.

It is easy to understand the rather skeptical attitude Paul Morand, moralist and friend of Proust, adopts as he makes his plaintiff's address to the year 1900: "Why did you make us believe in germs, electricity, the white race? Why the nest egg and low wages? Why did you bear your teeth at the slightest provocation and bequeath us war? Why were you so ugly, so rich and so happy?"

Minor discord or total disagreement? The end of the century sought to drown its shadows and shame in pleasure. Ugly, rich and happy. It only wanted to remember the two last adjectives... enclosed in an enormous Champagne bubble.

Ceramic vases with a "dragon-fly woman" pattern by D. Massier (Vallauris).

ART NOUVEAU ?
A CONVOLVULUS

This new art form triumphed at the World Exhibition... it spread its tendrils around the metro entrances which were just being installed along the first line linking Vincennes to Maillot. The famous wrought-iron entrances were the work of the architect Guimard who was one of the pioneers of *Art Nouveau*. An entire pavilion was set aside for it. In France, *Art Nouveau* was baptised « Modern Style », anglophile snobbery *oblige*, and Tiffany Style in the United States. It was also called noodle style, whip style and later on, *Belle Epoque* style...

How to define *Art Nouveau?* The creation of aesthetes, the converging of original personalities, painters: Bonnard and Mucha; decorative architects: Gaud, Guimard, de Feure, Majorelle, Vallin, André; sculptors: Maillol; art glass designers: Gallé, Daum, Tiffany, all promoters of a means of expression that was to mark the period. Posters, advertising, fashion, jewels, decoration, objets d'art and art itself were all to give way to the repeated onslaughts of these imaginative mandarins fascinated by Nature. "*Art Nouveau* basically took the form of decorative arts", wrote the art historian Bernard Champigneule.

"Woman was its symbol." Woman with her figure stylised by the corset. The vine woman. Undulations, convolutions, cascading curves... The meander explains all. It was the philosopher Henri Bergson who said so, and the visitors to the Exhibition could not believe their eyes.

Majorelle's wings

"The spiral is queen", explained Arthur Conte, "the line is not pure, the taste precious, all is undulating, diffuse, vaporous, cloudy. Every pretty woman must be a convolvulus, iris or gladiolus. The

Under the impetus of Jacques Descamps, the President of Perrier-Jouët, a collection of furniture and objects from the 1900's has been brought together to pay hommage to the Belle Epoque.
Below: desk by Majorelle. Opposite: showcase by Gauthier-Poinsignon, Majorelle's pupil.

skirt undulates, everything is convoluted, façades, halls, staircases: the Orsay Station and the Alexander III Bridge. Hector Guimard designed the Castel Béranger, rue La Fontaine and the first entrances to the Paris metro, using the same undulating lines. Majorelle's water-lily desk is set off by two wings. Gallé designed a table top in flower marquetry. The Pavilion of the Muses where Robert de Montesquiou lived is in a floral style. Armchairs are incrusted with wild rose leaves and dragonfly wings."

In his workshop in Nancy, Gallé was sculpting glassware decorated with plants. Mere fantasy? An extravagance to amuse a brillant but bored society? "Nothing could be further from the truth", states Bernard Champigneule. "Art Nouveau was the fruit of a belief and contemplation. The creation of a new style was a poetic belief and a philosophy, a movement of humanitarian thought."

Could not the more modest classes have the benefit of happier surroundings like the rich? The creators of this style were apostles who believed themselves invested with a social mission from which all severity would be totally banned.

Collection Perrier-Jouët

Furniture by the famous Parisian decorator Georges de Feure.

Opalescence and nuance: a vase by Gallé.

ÉMILE GALLÉ :
THE MASTER
GLASS-MAKERS'S FLASK

Who was Gallé? He could give style to a tomato. But what moved him most was the pure sheath of a snowdrop. Gallé (1846-1904) was a naturalist, a botanist, an artist seeking adventure. Gallé was first a member of the Lorraine Horticultural Society, where he did studies of plants and on the interior of flowers. He became Head of the School of Nancy. At the same time he was discovering Japanese and Chinese art.

Imagine him in the Lorraine countryside, his botanist's case slung over his shoulder, sketch book in hand, tracking down shrubs and flowers in the same way the musician Olivier Messiaen perceives the songs of birds and the sounds of the forest.

"The love of nature found among poets and artists since the Romantic period took a rather special turn for Gallé", wrote Bernard Champigneule. "We are no longer dealing with nature that inspires exalted or nostalgic emotions, but nature chosen for the details found in its fleeting vegetation. Details to be analysed, transposed and then locked in glass for all time." Such is the "Anemone" for Perrier-Jouët.

13

What was the raw material Gallé worked for his carafes, ewers and vases? It is commonly thought to be glass paste. In fact the glass-maker from Nancy never made anything using glass paste according to the historian Bernard Champigneule.

He used much more delicate techniques which consisted of super-imposing layers of different transparent glasses. The objects were blown and fired. Enamel powders were encased between layers or deposited on the surface and the subsequent vitrification caused che-mical reactions nuancing the colours and composing a material that would then be decorated with acid-etched designs.

Transparent, opalescent, shimmering, brilliant, Gallé played on an almost infinite palette of colours that were also used by the other master glass-worker Daum. Symbolist and landscapist, Gallé never stopped his creative work. First his famous vases decorated with quotations from the works of the poets Verlaine and Rimbaud, then furniture harbouring sculpted leaves and flowers, and innumerable

Here the Judean pitch is applied to those areas that are not to be etched by the acid.

*Glass-workers in the Gallé workshop
preparing crystal pieces (1913).*

other objects each distinctly recognisable as his craft yet each different from the other.

With fame, his influence and his methods spread far beyond the School of Nancy and his own workshop. Gallé became president of the School along with Daum, Majorelle and Vallin, an artistic cabinet-maker. It was not until near the close of the century, well after being awarded the grand prize at the 1889 World Exhibition, that he decided to found an industrial workshop, "driven by the desire common to many *Art Nouveau* artists to disseminate their work on a large scale". It was in the Nancy workshop that the Perrier-Jouët bottle with its floral design was first produced in 1900 upon a request by Henri Gallice who was responsible for the brand at the time.

Everywhere there is feasting, the Champagne flows. A painting by Jean Béraud.

1900
AND IT'S GAIETY

This period is also a turning point for Champagne and marked the beginning of a new area. From the "still wines" of before dom Perignon and up to the special vintages such as Perrier-Jouët's "Belle Epoque", Champagne ceased to be legend and became part of œnology. Although it was invented in the 17th Century, it is primarily a product of the 19th century, as the British historian Hugh Johnson points out. Most of the great Champagne houses were founded between 1780 and 1880.

Perrier-Jouët is no exception. It was founded in 1811 by a native of Epernay, Pierre-Nicolas-Marie Perrier, whose marketing and technological influence was to have a decisive effect. A century and a half of research and trial and error since dom Pérignon first invented Champagne: its colour had changed from grey to white — the colour of the limestone in the Champagne region which produces the poor soil from which springs this luxury wine.

In the 18th Century, Champagne was much loved by Madame de Pompadour and by Voltaire, but in the 1900's it became a favourite with the whole of France. In 1882, 36 million bottles were produced, one-quarter of which was for France and the remaining three-quarters for export. From 1850 to 1900 consumption in France quadrupled. It has continued to increase right up till today despite some poor harvests. It is true that in 1900 this sparkling wine had not really been democratised. Everyone has heard of it, and knows how to appreciate it, but it remains a luxury product reserved for important occasions, dinners and receptions.

Champagne has its fashions

Its cost no doubt explains why it was so infrequently served: a bottle was worth some ten to fifteen times the hourly wage of a worker. At Maxim's, a bottle of Perrier-Jouët brut cost 18 francs.

But the standard of living of the French was improving, France was moving into the Industrial Era and lifestyles were changing. François Bonal, the best connoisseur of Champagne and its region, writes that "consumption increased steadily from 1815, the *Restauration* and the Second Empire, but it was not drunk like it is today". "Champagne has its fashions too", notes the writer Armand Lanoux. "It reached international fame in 1900 but it would be necessary to take account of the Client's taste."

With dessert rather than as an aperitif

At the beginning of the century Champagne was drunk with dessert and not as an aperitif as it is today. The menus of the time are there to prove it. At the wedding reception of André Terrail, founder of the Tour d'Argent, and the daughter of Claudius Burdel, Champagne was the finishing note to the recital of the meal with its wines (see right hand page).

A columnist from "Le Figaro" noted that the 1904 Champagne was "miraculously golden". It was the crowning point of the meal which was why it had to be a sweet wine: with up to 300 grams of sugar per litre! The Russians, who hated dry wines, appreciated it. The British who were enlightened on the matter, protested at the addition of this sweet syrup. They wanted, and fought in unison for, the "dry". Perrier-Jouët soon felt from where the wind was blowing and was the first to reduce the addition of sugar; it did not change overnight but little by little transformed the taste of the wine.

Where could one drink Champagne in 1900? Wherever there was success and rejoicing. At the race course. In "Nana", Emile Zola describes the multitude of hampers filled with Champagne bottles on

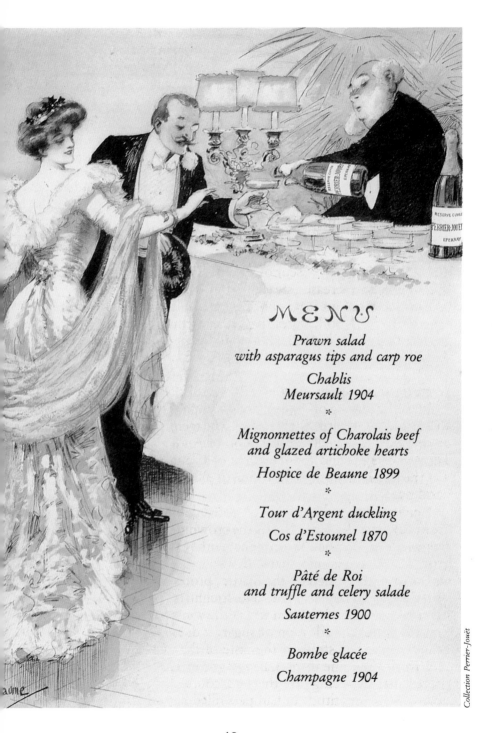

MENU

Prawn salad
with asparagus tips and carp roe

Chablis
Meursault 1904

*

Mignonnettes of Charolais beef
and glazed artichoke hearts

Hospice de Beaune 1899

*

Tour d'Argent duckling

Cos d'Estounel 1870

*

Pâté de Roi
and truffle and celery salade

Sauternes 1900

*

Bombe glacée

Champagne 1904

the day of the Grand Prix at Auteuil. At balls, too, Champagne flowed. The waltz and the Champagne cup (the round glass became increasingly popular from 1830 onwards) formed inseparable partners. François Bonal's mother liked Champagne so much that at the Bar-sur-Aube ball she would drink up to twelve glasses (the waiter counted them!).

The French consumed some 9 million bottles of champagne each year, most of which — the year is 1900 — were ordered in restaurants, fashionable night spots or at the bars of grand hotels where it was fashionable to be seen. Michel Budin, the Managing Director of Perrier-Jouët, recalls that at the time all the producers from Epernay and Reims placed the most emphasis on this type of clientele. "In 1900, restaurants were a prestige market accounting for the biggest volume in sales. Today they are largely only for prestige."

One great year in every three

From 1889 to 1914 the quality of vintages reached great heights. The historian André Simon points out the extreme concentration of good years and he speaks of the "golden age". François Bonal states, however, that the irregularity in vintages should not be forgotten and that "it is not until the 60's and 70's that a certain regularity is achieved in Champagne production".

Which are the great vintages of the *Belle Epoque?* 1889, 1892, 1893, 1899, 1900, 1904, 1906, 1911 and 1914. That is, one great year every three years over a period of a quarter of a century. This is still valid at the end of the 20th Century.

Here are the impressions of an expert wine taster, Michel Budin: 1889, high dosage, maderized (oxidized); 1892, low dosage, nervous; 1911, liquid gold, in 1960 a sheer master-piece; 1914, more lacey, finer than the 1911 vintage. (See page 59 for the commentated tasting by Jean-Luc Pouteau, best wine-waiter in the world).

A catastrophe named Phylloxera

1910 was a catastrophe with only half a million bottles. Half the Champagne vineyards, that is, 6 500 hectares were ravaged by Phylloxera. Was this to be the end of the most famous French vineyard? For many years it was believed that this small pest that had been attacking almost all European vineyards since 1860 would never dare plunge its sucker into the Champagne vine. Such a noble earth! The wine of the coronations in Reims. Such a thing was unthinkable. François Bonal quotes these words written by a journalist from the "Vigneron Champenois" in June 1880, "In Champagne there is not much concern about Phylloxera". In 1901 Phylloxera spread like gangrene throughout the Marne department; more than half the vines were infected.

American aid to combat the diabolical pest

Wine producers and dealers had to combine all their efforts to cut off the epidemic. The Champagne Viniculturist's Association was formed at Epernay. Various processes were developed including that of using carbon disulphide, and the intensive use of fertilizers; but the decisive step was the introduction of American plants which were grafted onto the Champagne vines. These successfully resisted the onslought of the diabolical pest. From this point on the vineyards were reconstructed, vines that had been infested with Phylloxera (one-third) were replaced by the grafted vines. Henceforth planting was done in battle array, the era of vines planted in clumps became a thing of the past with the new plantings in parallel lines.

As the gastronomic writer Raymond Dumay so rightly points out, destiny made Champagne a symbol of quality. While Maurice Holland concludes that Phylloxera taught vineyardists the need to unite and the advantages to be gained from solidarity. We are not far from the creation of the C.I.V.C. (Interprofessional Committee of Champagne Wines).

From the artisan industry at the beginning of the 20th Century, wine merchants and vineyardists were to fashion the organised industry we know today. The way was beset with revolts, uprisings and all kinds of difficulties and the fight for the product of the Champagne region was to be a long one. At the time officially recognised appellations did not exist but the concept, though it took a long time to materialise, was launched.

Exploding bottles

Exploding bottles were for a long time the bane of producers. In 1836 the invention by a chemist named François from Châlons-sur-Marne considerably reduced the amount of breakage. This pioneering œnologist discovered the amount of sugar that is to be added during the draw-off or *tirage* operation in order to form a fine foam but without breaking the bottle: this is known as the "François reduction method". At times 100% of the bottles filled exploded. In 1900

21

Let the Champagne flow, a song given at the "Concert Parisien".

breakage stabilised at 8%. As a result exports were better and greater: in 1900, 28 million bottles were exported.

The container had been perfected but what about the contents? Champagne lost neither quality nor identity through the grafts that the vines underwent. The wine's future is assured.

All that sparkles...

Which wine? Only that which comes from the Champagne region along the Marne river has the right to the appellation. Other wines from Saumur, Southern France and Algeria — transport by rail had a rôle to play — become "sparkling wines" by artificial processes. They are bought by wine merchants devoid of any scruples, detract from Champagne's image and the ancestral working methods of the Champagne vineyardists who are so attached to the authenticity of their production.

These "imported" wines are sold cheaply and fraud becomes patently obvious. Vineyardists are in fact penalised by the improper sale of their grapes and by the introduction of foreign wines. This led to the 1911 crisis which was called the Champagne Revolution.

"At the beginning of this century, the Champagne wine merchant was the only outlet for the vineyardist", writes Michel Budin. More was produced in 1900 than could be sold: 50 million actually produced as against the 26 million that were sold. Stocks were enormous and the merchants could not absorb all the producers' grapes. In some of the smaller holdings the vines were of only mediocre quality. Drastic selections were made to produce a Champagne of noble quality.

At last a victory over fraud

Merchants — at the time the word trader was used — were fully aware that they had to do something about this fraud. In 1903 along with 6000 vineyardists they signed a petition written by the Federation of Agricultural Unions requesting that only those municipalities of Reims, Epernay and Châlons be included in the Champagne region. The trend was towards the definition of a boundary for the region. Official measures were slow in coming, vineyardists grew impatient and anger was increasing at the wine presses. In 1907, 30 000 casks of wine were smuggled into Champagne only to be sent out labelled Ay and Cramant.

Since 1902 harvests had been poor. Disaster lurked around the corner, poverty and misery seemed to be the viniculturist's future lot.

In 1910 the Champagne Producer's Union wrote: "No calamity has been spared our unfortunate land: flood, storms, hail, mildew and Phylloxera". Protest meetings, tax strikes, barricades, pillaging: such was the climate in the vineyards in 1910, occupied by 40 000 troopers.

Finally, in February 1911, Parliament passed a law making it necessary to mention the words "Champagne" and "wine declared as produce of the Champagne region" on the label. All the sparkling wines produced in the Champagne region had to be made with grapes from the region. This was a great victory against fraud.

March 1911: Vineyardists demonstrating at Bar-sur-Aube. Tax returns are burnt before Mr Chautemps, the Under-Prefect.

But what about vineyardists from the Aube region and their 5 000 hectares of vines? These new rules barred them from the Champagne market. Where were they now to sell their harvests?

The Aube region, or Lower Champagne under the Old Regime, had been sacrificed, in the eyes of the people of Troyes, the historic capital of the Champagne counts. And in the eyes of history the people of Aube are just as much part of Champagne. Such, however, was not the view of the inhabitants of the Marne department. Backed by the fraud merchants, the inhabitants of Aube began their protests

in February 1911. Tax returns were burned in the streets, the municipal councils resigned, more than 5 000 vineyardists demonstrated in Troyes, their motto : "Win or die". Anger ran high as they shouted out their slogan: "Champagne was and always will be our region, and that is the way it shall be!"

Setting up a hierarchy of vintages

Finally, just a few months before the outbreak of World War I, the Aube vineyardists were authorised to sell their produce to the Marne merchants under the name of "second zone Champagne". This kindled yet another Marne-Aube feud. Only time was able to appease the rivalry between the regions. A vintage scale was introduced as a guide to the standard of the different wines. It remained unofficial until 1914. Merchants were fully aware that wines from Sillery, Ay, Ambonnay, Bouzy were superior to those from Bar-sur-Aube, but it was not until 1919 that the vintage scale became official and later still that prices for grapes per kilo were fixed by the profession.

By 1910 the basic techniques had been mastered. "We now know everything", said Dovaz. Œnologists and cellar masters are on the road to developing the "champenoise" method as it is practised today. "Sales are increasing, technology is changing", writes Michel Budin. In 1900 at Perrier-Jouët's, 200 people are required to ship one million bottles. Today, 70 people are enough for 2.4 million.

Science watches over the vintages

Everywhere mechanisation is taking over from man. Sorters, bottling machines using rotating siphons, semi-automatic corking machines make their entry into the wine cellar. Quality is monitored by œnologists: science watches over the vintages.

Increased care is taken during vinification. Champagne is placed in wooden vats. They know the amount of sugar needed for foam to develop, and disgorging using the freezing method becomes increasingly common after 1892. The apparatus for this cost 12 000 francs and was first installed at Moët et Chandon and Perrier-Jouët. The neck of the bottle is placed in a liquid at -10 or $-15\,^{\circ}C$ before disgorging.

Another innovation is the selection of yeasts — thank you Pasteur! — ensuring healthy fermentation thus avoiding all risk of insufficient foaming. The leading brand names then started to work the wine in the limestone caves in the region and not in their surface cellars, thereby producing a finer and longer-lasting bubble. Bottles became increasingly solid. In 1918, mechanical blowing was mandatory. Champagne lost its fragile glass wings and reinforced its wonderful sparkling bubbles. Tastes change... The dry or *brut* was to replace the sweet or semi-sweet and sweetened wines.

Confronted with competition from sparkling wines and whisky, the more prestigious Champagne houses grouped together to form a marketing union for Champagne wines with the aim of being present at the World Exhibitions in all the European capitals.

From Russia to America

Despite poor harvests, Champagne sold much better on the Belgian, Argentinian, Russian and German markets than in 1900. The English market had fallen by a third even though it was drunk as a luxury table wine by the upper classes and seen as a symbol of the "Entente Cordiale". The most significant market penetration was, however, in the U.S. It became, as in France, synonymous with pleasure. In New Orleans, for example, there was no stopping its tide... There still remained vast areas of the globe to be conquered.

Champagne, the Belle Epoque, some figures

Champagne production since the 18th century

Around 1715 (date of dom Pérignon's death): approx. 20 000 bottles
1789: from 300 000 to 500 000   1870: 17 million
1844: 6 600 000 (first statistics)   1900: 27 million

The leading names in 1900

Some thirty brand names dominated the market in 1900: Moët et Chandon, Perrier-Jouët, Pol Roger, Ayala, Krug, Clicquot, Mumm, Pommery, Lanson, Heidsieck, Bollinger... The surface area under cultivation was 11 681 hectares in 1913.

Sales (in bottles)

Years	France	Abroad
1889	1.1 million	19.1 million
1890	4.7 million	21 million
1900	7 million	20 million
1910	7 million	23 million

THE BOURGEOISIE HAS TIME FOR PLEASURE

Arthur Conte wrote: "In fact the *Belle Epoque* was epitomised by a bourgeoisie harking back to the pleasures of the Regency as though neither Revolution, nor Bismarck, nor Science had existed and as though other revolutions were not to come. The bourgeois simply replaced the nobleman. France had never been so prosperous. The festivities of the World Exhibition were being prepared in an atmosphere of unequalled calm. This exhibition was to give Paris the title of capital of Europe." At a time when Champagne and its region were undergoing severe growth crises, the festivities and the bubbling wine are inseparable. Alfred de Vigny wrote: "In the foaming wine of Ay glimmers a ray of happiness".

We are in the very heart of the myth of prosperity. Take for example the fabulous and extraordinary mayors' banquet given on September 22nd 1900 in the Tuileries Gardens for 22 000 mayors from the four corners of France. They swarmed under a sea of marquees under the bemused President of the Republic, Emile Loubet, and the President of the Council, Waldeck-Rousseau.

Here was a feast in Gargantuan style conceived by the Republican Left then in power: to reinforce its position, said the gazettes. The figures bear witness to that: 200 000 plates, 100 000 glasses, 50 000 bread rolls, 250 head of Nevers beef, 150 dozen ducklings from Rouen, 2 500 kilos of French beans, potatoes, kidney beans, 3 000 Bresse chickens: the pamphlet distributed to the personnel — 360 chefs — was 18 pages long!

A flood of liquids of all sorts: 20 000 bottles of Preignac, Saint-Julien and Margaux red, as many again of white Sauternes and 20 000 bottles of Champagne, all served by 200 wine waiters and brought to table by automobile! And this was at a time when there were still 1 367 omnibuses drawn through the streets of Paris by 17 000 horses...

Long live the Republic! Long live Monsieur Loubet! At the stroke of midday the "Marseillaise" rang out. Let's have a closer look at the feasting of the first citizens of France:

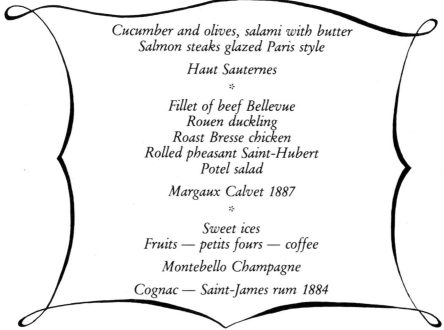

Cucumber and olives, salami with butter
Salmon steaks glazed Paris style

Haut Sauternes

*

Fillet of beef Bellevue
Rouen duckling
Roast Bresse chicken
Rolled pheasant Saint-Hubert
Potel salad

Margaux Calvet 1887

*

Sweet ices
Fruits — petits fours — coffee

Montebello Champagne

Cognac — Saint-James rum 1884

What was being celebrated? In the words of President Loubet: "the glorious memory of 1792 in the peace and joy of the Exhibition". Law and justice; the ovation is beyond measure: there is an overwhelming impression of plebiscite. The 12 chefs are presented to the President. The feast comes to an end, democracy has scored a point.

Edmond Rostand: a cup to the glory of Sarah Bernhardt.

THE NEW CULINARY ART OF ESCOFFIER

Mere chance? No. The talent of Auguste Escoffier (1847-1935), master cook, exploded right at the turn of the century. The *Belle Epoque* flowed with Champagne but it was also a cascade of festive foods. Escoffier's masterpiece, the "Guide Culinaire" with its 5 000 recipes, was published in 1903, a series of recipes and methods that was to influence several generations of chefs. He modestly subtitled his book "Practical memorandum of cooking practices". In the history of culinary methods, it can definitely be said that there are the pre- and post-Escoffier periods.

The son and grandson of blacksmiths from Villeneuve-Loubet near Nice, young Auguste was sent as cook's boy to his uncle's restaurant in Nice which had not yet been annexed to France. At the time he was thirteen and wanted to become a sculptor: "I had a taste for the arts" (unpublished memoirs). However destiny was to place him in the footsteps of his grandmother who was an "authentic cordon bleu whose precious recipes I have kept and which I have unhesitatingly used throughout my career".

After three years apprenticeship in Nice, the cook's boy went to Paris where he accepted a position as cook's helper in the Petit Moulin Rouge restaurant. This renowned establishment in avenue d'Antin no longer exists today. The year is 1865 and Auguste is nineteen. "It was not rare to meet members of French and foreign high society there. The Prince of Wales, the future Edward VII, used to dine in the company of Gambetta and other prominent members of political circles", he wrote in his "Mémoires".

To the glory of Gladiator

In his "Mémoires", Escoffier mentions a gala dinner offered by the comte de Lagrange after his horse Gladiator won the Grand Prix de Paris. The saddle of lamb was accompanied by a Château-Lafite 1846 followed by a Veuve Clicquot Champagne and then a Château-Yquem — the great white was flanked by two princes of the vine.

After being called up for military service in the war of 1870 (the menu was cat with a side dish of rat), his rise in the profession was to reach the dizzy heights of the art with glory as his final recompense.

By virtue of his talents as an organiser — manager we would say today — the son of the provençal blacksmith was given positions of great responsibility (financial and other) which had never before been given to a chef. The bourgeois Escoffier was to become the right-hand man of César Ritz, the inventor of the modern hotel industry.

From the Savoy to the Ritz

Escoffier judiciously notes that the Savoy Hotel and its restaurant soon became a school of modern hotel practice and the centre of development for French *cuisine* in England.

The menus were written in French in accordance with Escoffier's directives. He introduced dinners at a fixed price — a stroke of genius. Clients had full confidence in him. And the chef had full liberty to serve whatever he chose, an innovation that had never been seen before and which "is the best stimulant for the creative imagination". Is this not what the young revolutionaries of *nouvelle cuisine* are doing today? Escoffier cooked for Emile Zola at the highly select Savoy when the writer "came to London to study the customs of the city's slums. He was highly partial to gastronomy and raw sardines".

In honour of the singer Nellie Melba he created the pêche Melba "which is comprised solely of tender, perfectly ripe peaches, vanilla ice-cream and sweet raspberry purée".

After the Grand Hotel in Rome, Ritz and Escoffier opened the Carlton in London and finally the Ritz in Paris in company with "Monsieur Olivier", the director of the Palace and who had been able to win the favours of a difficult client in the person of Marcel Proust.

Food for stars

Escoffier, a man of distinction and exactitude in a bowler hat, ruled from his impeccably neat office in the immense basement kitchens of these palaces that were the "homes" of the international upper classes.

The feared and revered master was in charge of dozens of sauce cooks, dessert cooks, grillers, pastry cooks, larderkeepers, apprentices and cook's boys all of whom tackled the *foie gras au porto*, the *chaud-froid Jeannette*, the *mousseux d'écrevisses*, the *cuisse de nymphe Aurore* (frogs legs specially prepared for the Prince of Wales), the *salade Réjane*, the *mignonnettes de cailles Rachel*, the *filets de sole Coquelin*, the *selle d'agneau Edouard VII*, the *poires Mary Garden* and the *fraises Sarah Bernhardt...* Regal dishes dedicated to women, the finest for those upon whom fortune had smiled without whom the little cook's boy from Nice would never have been able to dazzle his fellows nor hand down his capital culinary ideas.

Creator and pedagogue

Not only was Escoffier an authentic creator but he also codified the basis of 20th Century *cuisine*. Anti-establishment, a trifle provocative, the new chefs first had to digest Escoffier's teachings, for he was first and foremost an unparalleled pedagogue.

"He brought some order to the conglomeration of a gastronomy cluttered with any number of sauces", writes Raymond Olivier another great teacher of international standing. A man of brilliant ideas, though promoter of somewhat outmoded styles — like partridge and truffle soufflé — this Provençal of London sought to rationalise the obscure tasks in the kitchen, dividing them up and distributing them among the brigade according to well-defined "parts" (fish, meats, sauces...). There were 120 people employed in the Savoy kitchens, a veritable army of chefs! Without his order and method there would have been nothing.

Escoffier was a visionary who foresaw that French *cuisine* had to evolve with the people and their life style. He banished heavy sauces and gave emphasis to the natural juices of meat, fish and vegetables and light stocks. He lived before his time and died poor in 1935.

Detail from a caricature of couples by Cardona ("Le Rire", 1907).

CHEZ MAXIM'S AND THE GLORY OF CHAMPAGNE

From the Tuileries Gardens, cross over the Place de la Concorde to the Rue Royale and on to Maxim's, the "temple to Champagne", as François Bonal calls it. One anecdote says that a delegation of peasant mayors sat down on the terrace which no longer exists. They were soon sent on their way by an impolite doorman. Mayor or not, these were just "bumpkins". For not just anyone enters this most famous restaurant in the world. Even then! This was told by the *maître d'hôtel* Hugo who ruled from 1899 to 1919.

This former coachman's café which was renovated in 1893 by Maxime Gaillard was experiencing formidable success. The great Russian Dukes (the real ones), the merry bands of *demi-mondaines* (the beautiful Otéro), acknowledged princes (Murat), the money princes (Lebaudy, nick-named the little sugar-bowl), lettered men-about-town (Pierre Louÿs), society people (Boni de Castellane) and all those who dreamed of more or less eccentric pleasures adopted the ground and upper floors (private rooms) of this former ice-cream vendor's which, in 1893 on the same day as the Prix de Diane, became a cabaret for the "labourers of pleasure, a necessary breed", in the words of one satisfied reveller. All the celebrities of the century were to haunt Maxim's. It even happened that some fashionable authors drew their inspiration here, for example, Georges Feydeau for "The Lady from *Chez Maxim's*". The cork-popping wine, as it was termed, was always present at these parties.

Sup for just one louis

Here is what René Héron de Villefosse, the historian of Parisian restaurants, has to say about Maxim's: "The 1900 Exhibition consecrated Maxim's in its international reputation. No foreigner of any importance who had come to visit the giant Exhibition missed coming to sup at Maxim's. At 10 o'clock in the evening the doors were closed in order to better serve the late-night diners. It was possible to dine for one louis and even much less as the owner, Cornuché, allowed the aristocracy credit which flattered the American clients."

Here is a 1900 menu with prices: hors d'œuvre, 75 centimes; oysters from Ostende, 3,5 francs a dozen; small lobsters in *court-bouillon*, 2,50 francs; sole, Polignac style, 2 francs; veal scallop, Viennese style, 2,25 francs; grain-fed chicken casserole, 6 francs.

The menu for the 1906 New Year's Eve party was 50 francs: marrow *croustade*, stuffed chicken American style, *foie gras au porto*, salad, New Year ice-cream; not a sign of lobster or caviar, the "musts" of a New Year's eve party today.

At the bar or at table, it's as you wish

And the wine? The wine-list was twenty four pages long with 842 different wines. Champagne was drunk at the bar by the men and at table by the society ladies who had to put up with the giggling cocottes just a few glances away, roused to giddy gaiety by the Epernay and Reims wine. Gay, gay, be gay! The wine that sparkles and amuses, sweet to taste, "Caucasian" writes Armand Lanoux. It is the king of desserts: the moment everyone waited for to "chop off its head" and pass around the glasses.

Alex Humbert was born in 1905, his father was a Burgundian. He was to become the greatest chef at Maxim's spending twenty years in the kitchens there. It was he who gradually composed the symphony of Maxim's menu: sole Albert, fatted chicken with cucumber, Belle Otéro crêpes. In the great restaurants of the time, the Café de la Paix, the Goncourts' Drouant, Proust's Ritz, The Grand Hôtel where

Zola's Nana was to die, Lucas at the Madeleine decorated with Majorelle's magnificient wood panelling, Champagne was only served during the last act, as the curtain came down, after the Sauternes and just before the brandy. That was its place... by ritual.

At the Ritz, for a menu called "Triumph of Gastronomy", as the gourmet reached the end of his pilgrimage, there appeared an 1899 Yquem and a 1904 Clicquot Mathusalem just before the fine Champagne, Chartreuse or Grand Marnier.

Place of honour in the houses of dishonour

Let's track down the gold-capped wine in Paris. Its aphrodisiac qualities were praised and so it took place of honour in the houses of dishonour, brothels giving vent to all fantasies, the Chabanais, the Sphinx, the One Two Two, and the Palais Oriental in Reims where it is said that more Champagne was drunk than in all the town's other restaurants and cafés.

At the Folies-Bergères it is the number one pick-me-up. And in the Montmartre bars it accompanies the roudy nights: the night-time revellers call for Champagne and kisses. Champagne is the essence of joy, say the first advertisements.

COCKTAILS HAVE ALREADY COME TO THE PARTY

An essence for mixing: the cocktail in its embryonic form. The iconoclastic Russians were already having strange concoctions made up for themselves which Maxim's purist Hugo found quite "crazy". They used whisky, peach nectar and Champagne. The sweeter it was, the better they liked it. Peach nectar without the whisky was to become one of the most frequent partners of Champagne as in the famous "Bellini" invented in Venice by the barman at the Excelsior. But Jules Romain wrote that in 1908 whisky-Champagne was still being served at the Closerie des Lilas in Paris.

The light-hearted Poirot of Champagne cocktails, Alphonse Allais, has collected innumerable recipes in his book "Le Captain Cap" (1902). His favourite, the "Pick-me-up", is made of lemon juice, grenadine, kirsch and Champagne, an invigorating mixture. A real thirst-quencher is the Champagne Julep with mint and rum; the Champagne Gobbler is a symphony of ingredients: curaçao, walnut cream, Saint-Marceaux tisane, a slice of orange and one of lemon, fruits in season with a dash of red port. What a whirlwind! The oldest of these bubbly mixtures is still Champagne Punch. François Bonal has found a letter written by one of Casanova's mistresses in 1740. She says: "You can't imagine how gay we grew after having drunk of the Champagne Punch". Mixed with cognac and pineapple and served piping hot after having been warmed in a *bain-marie*, this punch of the 1890's was a veritable magic potion.

Always sparkeling...

The Black Velvet or Champagne Velvet
Into a 33 cl glass, pour: 15 cl of chilled stout (Guiness, Murphy, Beamisch) and 15 cl of chilled brut Champagne. Do not mix.

Champagne Cocktail
Put a lump of sugar in a tulip glass and pour a few dashes of Angostura bitters onto it. Add a half measure (2 cl) of cognac. Fill the glass with chilled Champagne. Decorate with a slice of orange and a glacé cherry.

Champagne Julep
Crush a few leaves of fresh mint with a spoonful of sugar. Put into a Champagne flute. Add chilled Champagne. Decorate with a branch of fresh mint.

Cloud Buster
Put one measure (4 cl) of vodka into a tulip glass. Add three ice cubes. Fill with Champagne. Present with a spiral of lemon rind.

The Eagle
Pour one measure (4 cl) of imperial mandarine liqueur into a Champagne flute or tulip. Fill with chilled brut Champagne.

CHAMPAGNE AND FINE CUISINE

With the exception of the *potée champenoise* and pigs' trotters Sainte-Menehould style served with split peas (somewhat rustic dishes), the Champagne region itself offers little in the way of gastronomic delights. It has, however, contributed its wine to complement and refine certain dishes. Dom Perignon's liquor has been used to give a different dimension to the fare of royalty.

Ever since Carême, Champagne has gained steadily in favour as one of the secret ingredients in the alchemy of the great chefs. Fillets of salmon and shrimps in Champagne, carp Chambord style, all these dishes are served with the divine Champagne sauce that was originally served for the first time in 1815 with casseroled fillets of sole. The turbot *à la royale* and Rothschild salmon require four bottles of Champagne; these are all classics from the beginning of the century as is the famous fatted chicken in Champagne.

"Drink a flute of well-chilled Champagne as you are preparing the dish", suggests the best chef in Reims, Gérard Boyer, of the Château Crayères. Here are a few of the more famous recipes using Champagne.

Salmon cooked in Champagne

Cut some thick salmon steaks. Butter an oven-proof dish and line it with finely chopped shallots and a mixture of diced vegetables. Lay the salmon steaks on this bed and moisten half-way with an equal mixture of fish stock and Champagne. Cook in a preheated oven at 225°C. Drain and keep warm. Strain the cooking juices and add some cream (1 dl for 2.5 dl of juices) and reduce by half. Check the seasoning. Add a large piece of butter cut into small pieces and beat. Coat the steaks with this sauce.

Fatted chicken in Champagne aspic

Salt and pepper the inside and outside of a chicken weighing approximately 1.750 kg and brown it on all sides in a stewing pan. Add diced carrot, turnip, leek, celery, onion and mushroom stalks and a *bouquet garni*. Cover and place on a high flame for about 45 minutes turning the chicken from time to time so that it cooks on all sides. Remove the lid, add half a bottle of Champagne, stir and finish cooking with the lid off. Prepare an instant aspic using the rest of the Champagne. Strain the cooking juices and add to the aspic. Allow the chicken to cool completely, carve it into pieces and arrange them on a serving dish. Coat with the aspic and allow to set in the refrigerator. Re-coat the dish with aspic twice more.

Brill cooked in Champagne

Prepare the whole brill, and surround with 24 small, cleaned mushrooms and add an equal quantity of Champagne to the fish stock: the fish should be just covered. Bring to the boil and then transfer to the oven to finish cooking basting the fish several times. Drain. Put the fish on a serving plate white skin upwards and keep warm. Reduce the cooking juices by half. Bind this sauce with a good spoonful of softened butter, letting it bubble gently. Add 50 g of butter, mix and strain. Remove the white skin from the brill, coat with the sauce. It can be garnished with small fillets of sole.

Champagne sorbet

Take 75 cl of Champagne, 40 cl of water and 250 g of sugar. Make a syrup with the water and sugar, allow to cool and mix in the Champagne. This sorbet is very delicate and so should only be placed in the sorbetière 20 minutes before it is to be served.

The anenome bottles lie in cellars 9 km long.

THE WORLD
AND THE WONDER
OF CHAMPAGNE

Just a little over a decade into the century: 1811. Engraved above the entrance to *Perrier-Jouët*, avenue de Champagne at Epernay, this date commemorates two events: the birth of Napoleon's son and that of a great name in Champagne, Perrier-Jouët or the Gallé flower Champagne. Here is how intuition, inventions and a marketing strategy of reliability with a touch of the fanciful have contributed to the rapid rise of this name.

The destiny of Pierre-Nicolas-Marie Perrier-Jouët, founder of the brand name, was to take a different turn because of this wine that Napoleon liked so much. This upper class family manufactured corks like those invented by dom Pérignon himself in Hautvillers around 1680 and sold them to the merchants in the Champagne region.

While the father laid the foundations, it was the son Charles Perrier who undertook to develop the name, especially in England, then under the reign of Queen Victoria, whose court loved to refresh itself with Perrier-Jouët. It was also the favourite Champagne of Edward VII. The links that had been made by the founding father between Perrier-Jouët and the United Kingdom became stronger over time. In the 19th Century the royal taste buds on the other side of the Channel had already become highly sensitive. A man of contacts and a skilful businessman, Charles Perrier's success was so outstanding that he was elected mayor of Epernay toward the middle of the century.

The Champs-Elysées of Champagne

An eminent member of the community, Charles Perrier lived in what was to become the Perrier castle, a strange building of curved architecture in a baroque style which now houses the Epernay library. On the other side of this prestigious avenue, the "Champs-Élysées of Champagne", stands the 18th Century private hotel with its harmonious square courtyard which was the business house of Perrier-Jouët; below it are 9 km of cellars.

He had no descendants and so he chose one of his nephews, Henri Gallice. He was the founder and first president of the Champagne Viniculturists' Association.

In 1900 Perrier-Jouët was producing one million bottles and the name figures among the few greats in Champagne which have world renown. It was through the efficiency of the leaders from the Champagne region that, under the Second Empire, the favourite wine of Madame de Pompadour was given its brand name.

A vineyard of noble origins

The "trump card" of Perrier-Jouët is its 100 hectare vineyard whose yield covers 40% of the firm's requirements. It is a fine vineyard distributed through the great vintages of Avize (100%, 6 ha), Cramant (100%, 30 ha), two jewels of the land for the Chardonnay vine.

The remainder of their vineyards are *pinot noir* at Ay (100%, 10 ha), at Mailly (100%, 10 ha), and Dizy (95%, 10 ha) as well as 10 hectares at Vinay (86%) for the *pinot meunier* and 21.5 hectares at Orbais (83%). This vineyard was gradually set up by Pierre-Nicolas-Marie Perrier-Jouët from 1840 onwards. He was an inspired man, the jewel of his collection is the 40 hectares on the *côte des blancs*, the Olympus of Champagne in the heart of the Cramant vineyards, half-way up the slopes: at the top it is too damp, at the bottom the risk of frost is too great.

At the time Pierre-Nicolas-Marie Perrier-Jouët was not aware that the wine from the *côte des blancs* was to produce a Champagne of refined elegance and liveliness, the one for which Champagne lovers reserve their greatest praise today. There are great differences of taste between the Champagne of the *Restauration* period, that of the Second Empire, and the diaphanous, nervous wine savoured at the end of the 20th century.

Choice of a visionary of modern œnology, these 40 hectares are priceless. The quality of a Champagne depends on the quality of the grapes, the raw material to be vinified into wine as Pierre Ernst, one of the managers at Perrier-Jouët, points out.

The role of the master glass-maker

Champagne's prestige is also due to its splendour and beauty. In 1902, Henri Gallice has the idea of ordering a bottle decorated with an arabesque of anemones from the illustrious art glassworker, Emile Gallé. This bottle will never stop contributing to Perrier-Jouët's renown. Historically, Gallé's bottle came after the Emperor's carafe blown by Mercier for Napoleon III and after Rœderer's famous crystal flask made for the Tsar of Russia.

Others such as Pol Roger and Henriot, designed decorated bottles at the turn of the century but only the bottle by the master glass-maker chosen by Perrier-Jouët has lasted beyond the Belle Epoque.

One day in 1964, Pierre Ernst found four "Belle Epoque 1900" bottles in a cupboard in a winecellar in Epernay, one of which was broken. The entire past of Perrier-Jouët was suddenly conjured up. One of these original bottles was remodelled and used for the seventieth birthday celebrations of Duke Ellington at the Alcazar in Paris in 1966. For two years Maxim's and Fauchon had the exclusive right to its sale.

The Modern Style delights the gourmet elite

The idea of commercializing Gallé's bottle was more than just appealing. Michel Budin, a descendant of one of the founders, has been running Perrier-Jouët with his strict business sense since 1959. Not content with simply having Gallé's bottle reproduced by a glass enamelist, he demanded that the capsules be identical with the original ones and that matching tulip glasses be made. In 1965 there was only one master glass-maker capable of vitrifying at 600°C.

"There is no doubt as to the aesthetic and marketing success of the Gallé bottle", writes the historian Michel Dovaz in his "Encyclopedia of Champagne"; Michel Budin adds that "it is a tremendous hit in the United States with 30% of sales in 1984. The Modern Style simply delights the gourmet elite".

Gallé's flower, today on all tables.

THE ARTISAN
FROM ARGENTEUIL,
GLASS AND FRIENDSHIP

How to reproduce this bottle, relic of a time almost fifty years past? Gallé's workshop has closed, the prosperity of the genius glass-maker did not long outlive the master, or rather it was stifled by the arrival of new art forms. Art replaces art. There were plenty of art glass-makers and the management of Perrier-Jouët set off to visit them with their historic bottle in hand. Everywhere they met with the same reply: impossible to recreate the design in relief, the enamel scales would peel off under the effect of the heat (600°C).

The men from Perrier-Jouët refused all compromise on the stylised anemone relief design. They wanted to feel them on the bottle just as they were originally invented by the naturalist wizard from Nancy.

The challenge was finally taken up by a small artisan glass-worker living in the Paris suburbs, Jean Bigou. He was a water-colour painter educated at the Beaux-Arts. It was by a chance friendship that he was brought into contact with Pierre Ernst in the middle of the 60's. Ernst was determined that his project of relaunching the Gallé bottle into the world of Champagne lovers should see the light of day.

Jean Bigou's hidden dream is to work with enamels. He paints folkloric costumes and rhymes on glasses which he then fires in an oven installed in his workshop garage. He makes the glasses by the dozen, his oven will not hold more. Orders come from retailers who have heard of his art; but only in infinitely small quantity. "Enamels in relief, I'll try it", said Jean Bigou to Pierre Ernst in 1965 when he showed him the Gallé bottle.

Thanks to Pablo Picasso's motto

He starts experimenting. He fires the bottle with its enamel design in several stages. He applies the successive layers of enamel driven by the idea of lowering the melting point so that the enamel can adhere. The bottles break by the dozen. Bigou finds himself confronted with an obstacle, but he perseveres. In this Pablo Picasso's motto helps him: "I seek not, I find".

Then one morning, he tries a neutral flux which he mixes into the enamel powders. One layer, two layers of enamels, flux, another layer: by virtue of successive mixtures, he was able to develop a scientific (and secret) dosage which worked.

Victory at last! The humble artisan from Argenteuil had passed through to the other side of the mirror. Mad with joy, Pierre Ernst has 5000 bottles delivered to Bigou who fires them in his two ovens... Gallé's discovery was to live again. And on a grand scale.

Tulip glasses bloom too

From 1965 to 1975, production rose from 5 000 bottles a year to 15 000. Jean Bigou suggested that Perrier-Jouët's labels be made of enamel also. This was, however, refused by the C.I.V.C. In order to meet this giant step forward, Perrier-Jouët decided to finance the technical installations. The problem is simple. All Bigou needs is ovens and workshops to produce all the *Belle Epoque* bottles for Perrier-Jouët. Demand for these is increasing all the time. Louis Vaudable, the head of Maxim's, demanded the exclusive right to the first *Belle Epoque* vintage.

The 500 000 bottles mark has now been reached. Bigou is now in his sprightly seventies and has passed on the flame to his two daughters both educated at art school. Like father, like daughters.

Driven on by the demands of Perrier-Jouët, Bigou's only big client, the two daughters bought a small house next to the station of Argenteuil and there in the garden they built a workshop which is much

The anenome garland as Gallé invented it.

more elaborate and in which they have five ovens each with a capacity of 378 bottles as well as the famous tulip glasses. In the 80's, Perrier-Jouët decided to launch a *Belle Epoque rosé* vintage.

A new challenge for Jean Bigou. He started by trying to tint the white bottle pink. Failure. One morning he got the idea of adding some pink powder to his enamel and flux mixture. Success.

Despite the number of bottles to be decorated and fired, the technique is still manual and the Bigous are closer to the artisans of the 19th Century than to modern industrialists.

"Waiter with fleur de Champagne", painting by Guy Buffet.

FROM THE BELLE ÉPOQUE TO TODAY

An interview with Michel Budin

You are, Michel Budin, the Managing Director of Perrier-Jouët, could you give us a brief outline of its history since the end of the 1914-18 war up to today? How did the brand develop over the first half of the century after the dizzy heights of the *Belle Epoque?*

M. Budin — In the years following the First World War, Perrier-Jouët retained all its prestige and renown. From the point of view of volume, it was far from the peaks reached during the last decade of the 19th Century, production had fallen.

- Could you explain?

M. B. - When the Dreyfus affair first flared up, production was at around one million bottles, even more, one million two hundred thousand. Why did sales drop? The owner at that time, Henri Gallice, was confronted with very keen competition in Great Britain from poor quality brands (wines that were not from Champagne).

He chose to let sales fall rather than lower the quality of Perrier-Jouët. He withdrew 600 000 bottles from the market between 1900 and 1910. This was no mean figure, being about 50% of production.

- A very courageous attitude?

M. B. - Yes, and one showing modern foresight. The company suffered. Only the brut and vintage production was maintained. When you think that up to 800 000 bottles were sold to the English, that was almost two thirds of its turnover.

- How can this favouritism for Perrier-Jouët be explained?

M. B. - Because Charles Perrier and his father were good wine-makers and clever salesmen. Firstly, the Perrier-Jouët dry Champagnes. These were greatly appreciated on the other side of the Channel. And Perrier-Jouët had the good fortune to use an excellent agent, a Burgundian named Boursot. This was a great asset, the Boursot family was Perrier-Jouët's agent in the U.K. from 1829 to 1945. The centenary of this collaboration was celebrated in 1929!

- You think that it was thanks to the Boursots that Perrier-Jouët was one of the leading Champagnes in the United Kingdom?

M. B. - The Boursots only handled Perrier-Jouët and they had introduced it everywhere. From 1840 onwards, the success of the name never ceased to grow. The 1874 Perrier-Jouët was one of the most expensive Champagnes ever sold at Christies in London. Up until 1914, this vintage held the record of the highest bid.

- It was your father who took over from Henri Gallice after the 1914-1918 war.

M. B. - Henri Gallice had been at the head of Perrier-Jouët since 1878. He had taken over from Charles Perrier. After the First World War and following the quality crisis in England, Gallice wanted to withdraw. He no longer felt motivated. He sold part of the capital to my family: Henri Gallice's son had married my mother's eldest sister. The Budin family asked my father to take charge of Perrier-Jouët as manager. He accepted and new horizons were opened up.

- Was your father already in the Champagne business?

M. B. - When he was 25 he started working at Delbeck's in Reims, a business that was bought out by Piper Heidsieck. My father was wounded in 1914 and took over the company in 1917. It was a strange time to be working in Champagne. In Epernay, the cellars, buildings and roofs were all in poor condition. He had to form new teams so that the company could prosper and develop. The 1919-1939 period was not a very prosperous one for Champagne. A crisis in 1919, another in 1921, sales fluctuated considerably and then they climbed until the 1928 crisis, the Wall Street crash in 1929 and mounting international tension until 1939. That is the historical setting.

- And at Perrier-Jouët?

M. B. - The problem was that it hadn't found an entry into the French market. It was precisely the domestic market that counted during the between-war period. The export market was experiencing serious difficulties. The United States was closed because of prohibition until 1935-36, Russia was emerging from feudality. Germany and Austria were undergoing peculiar ups and downs. Italy was out of the running, so what was left? Great Britain, Switzerland, Belgium and a handful of small markets: British colonies — Malta, India, Singapore, Egypt — Poland, for which everyone was fighting.

- Did your father orient his strategy towards private clients or restaurants?

M. B. - The main line of his policy was directed at restaurants that he managed to enter using the tactics of the day: give buyers certain advantages, extended payment dates, deposits on bottles, one case given free for every six or twelve delivered.

- And I suppose it was his wish to be seen in those restaurants that sold or could sell Perrier-Jouët?

M. B. - Of course. All the heads of Champagne houses were, and still are, excellent clients of restaurants. My father gave preference to London. He dined at the most chic restaurants quite regularly. He went to a different hotel each trip: the Savoy, the Claridge, the

Mayfair, the Dorchester (just opened) and the Barclay. It was here that best sales were to be made. The most Champagne was drunk there and in banquets and then, via the wine merchants, by private individuals.

- Do you have any figures for sales in Great Britain during your father's time?

M. B. - 150 000 to 200 000 bottles per year which was about 40 to 50% of Perrier-Jouët's production. At the time, some 400 000 to 500 000 bottles were sold depending on the harvests. In 1984, we are up to over two million.

- Has Perrier-Jouët always been a leader in famous brand Champagnes?

M. B. - No. Perrier-Jouët lost its position as leader when it stopped selling the poorer quality wine, what they call B.O.B. in the U.K., the Champagne that is labelled according to the buyer's wishes. Perrier-Jouët refused to sell Perrier-Jouët labelled "Savoy".

- You wanted to remain a great brand that is bought for its prestige?

M. B. - Yes. You must not overlook the fact that a great Champagne is still a luxury product. Back in the fifties I can remember arguing with the Director of the Savoy that French Champagne had dropped by 20% in comparison to the thirties. He showed me a 1938 wine list on which we saw that the vintages were 15% more expensive than the best Bordeaux wines. On a current wine list, however, the situation was reversed. "By Jove, you're right!" he exclaimed, dumbfounded. Champagne was just beginning to become democratised.

- What sort of a man was your father?

M. B. - From his physical aspect and his way of dressing, he looked an Englishman. In London people mistook him for an Englishman, especially since he spoke perfect English.

- Did he bring you up to think that you would one day be at the head of Perrier-Jouët?

Michel Budin, thirty-six years service to Champagne.

M. B. - By the time I was ten I was bilingual. My sisters and I had an English nanny which meant that I could actually read English before French. In 1940, I was fifteen. After the Liberation, he pushed me into doing the French equivalent of an M.B.A., at the same time I read for law. After a period in 1944-45 during which I was called up, he sent me to England to work for an auditor. Following that I underwent a ten-month training session in the Epernay cellars.

- A training session in the cellars?

M. B. - I worked in the cellars, not at Perrier-Jouët, but at Ayala where I was not known. Bringing in the harvest, riddling, disgorging, labelling the bottles. For sixty hours a week — that is the way to learn the vineyardist's trade. In the United States I came up against the wine merchant trade. For all wines. I drank. I drank a lot to compare.

- You are reputed among the closed circle of great Champagne producers to have an excellent "nose", of being a genius blender. Was it your father who passed on to you the secrets of Perrier-Jouët's production?

M. B. - I started working at Perrier-Jouët in 1949 when I was twenty-four. In the years 1941-1942, my father always invited me to tastings. I listened to his comments and trained my palate. A characterless, superficial wine or a full, fruity wine like our Cramant, the diamond of the Perrier-Jouët vintages. I learned how to compare, to determine the differences, the signs of taste intelligence. In 1951, challenged by a dealer from Tours who put three magnums in front of me, I was able to distinguish the magnum of wine from Loir-et-Cher from the two others which were a white from Aube and another from

Aisne. I must say that during my stay in the United States I had occasion to recognise French wines, to select and judge their vintage. I was the only French person and had the reputation of a connoisseur...

- You are an ace of vintages, but in fact you have certain reference points, you know where your wines come from, the classification of the different vintages and you also know when you have had to buy grapes to complement your own supplies. You do not just blend unknowingly.

M. B. - Depending on where the grapes come from, we can guess what the vintage will be like. That is why we have to maintain a certain regularity in what we buy so as to respect the floral style of the name. The Perrier-Jouët style is very special and is based on the origin of the grapes and the vinification of certain vintages. Not just any. What we buy are basically grapes that we want to vinify ourselves in Epernay for a better homogeneity. We take the same care with the entire harvest. Wines bought in bulk are less reliable.

- The only variations are due to the grapes themselves, the year is probably more or less explicit.

M. B. - The first thing would be to taste our vintages. What are they like? What are their qualities? And their faults? How will we dose the wine? That is where the vintage will be refined, when we try to blend different elements so as to obtain the best quality and by staying as close as possible to the Perrier-Jouët style. In 1959 and 1972, whatever we tried to do, we were far from it...

- It was you who introduced the vat instead of the barrel, even while your father was still head?

M. B. - Indeed! That was the only time there was any friction between us during the ten years we worked together. He was very reticent. It was not that he especially liked wood, he was afraid of the result when going from one to the other. We were going into the unknown. I suggested that we experiment. Over five years part of the vintage would be vinified in vats and the other in wood. We would taste and see the difference. The results were excellent. Since the 60's there has been practically no more Champagne in barrels.

- In 1959 you had sole responsability of the vintage. An important first. How did you feel, were you apprehensive?

M. B. - That's an understatement! You feel the whole weight of the name on your shoulders. I might even say on your nose... The 1959 vintage was not an easy one. It was a very ripe year with a lot of alcohol which is something that Champagne does not like. We harvested wines with 14° at Cramant. The best level is around 10° reinforced by light addition of sugar. Above 11°, more powerful and fruity, it is better suited for table wine than Champagne. The 1959 vintage was long in ripening. It lacks finesse.

- Which are the vintages that you are proudest of?

M. B. - In my opinion: 1961; 1964; 1966 which keeps well in a cellar; 1969 and 1971 were good years; 1973 was outstanding, magnificent; 1975 was good but a bit disappointing now; 1976 which is now at its best.

- What is a great vintage?

M. B. - One that gets past the ten year mark without changing. Twelve or fifteen years is even better.

- You don't have to wait ten years?

M. B. - No, but the years refine a wine, especially when it has exceptional qualities like the 1955 vintage.

Michel Budin is in his sixties, lively, cultivated, a great reader and of a pragmatic nature. He is responsible for the vintages at Perrier-Jouët, Mumm and Heidsieck Monopole. There are few people in Champagne who combine so many responsabilities. It represents the trifle of nearly 13 million bottles a year!

Opposite: Diploma awarded to Perrier-Jouët in San Francisco in 1894 during an international exhibition.

Collection Perrier-Jouët

From right to left: Jean-Luc Pouteau, Michel Budin, André Baveret, Pierre Ernst and Nicolas de Rabaudy.

THE BELLE ÉPOQUE VINTAGES

Extraordinary tasting
of Perrier-Jouët Champagnes
by Jean-Luc Pouteau,
world champion wine-waiter

In the presence of M. Budin: Managing Director, M. Ernst: Assistant Managing Director, M. Baveret: cellar master, M. de Rabaudy: gastronomic journalist, and M. Pouteau: world champion wine waiter, wine waiter at the Pavillon Elysée and responsible for wine purchases in the Gaston Lenôtre group. The aim of this tasting was to judge the lasting qualities of Perrier-Jouët Champagne from the *Belle Epoque*. About ten bottles were selected. M. Baveret, the cellar master, prepared the bottles taking a thousand precautions. He brought them up from the cellars where they had been since they were first laid there — a "paradise" away from the curious eyes of visitors, and above all from the light and any movement. What was in store for us in these venerable bottles? A fleeting instant of joy followed by a rapid oxidation would have not surprised us. Such was not the case, quite the contrary.

Perrier-Jouët 1893
Clear golden cloak, still full of very fine, small bubbles which lasted for more than a minute... Slightly rancid nose with the aroma of very

One hundred and sixty years old: a bottle of rare exception.

ripe fruit (apple, quince), a lot of aromatic intensity. Good lead, very brut, very dry, full. The gas is still there, long in the mouth, but at the end leaves a slightly bitter taste. Extraordinary performance.

Perrier-Jouët 1900
Still sparkling, clear gold colour. Nose less strong than the 1893 with different aromas, tending more toward blooming white roses. Under the effect of the air tended to faded rose. Very beautiful floral flavour but also fruity. Rich, strong wine. Very powerful, splendid astringency, still a lot of freshness. Under the effect of the air (one hour) slight odour of torrefaction and toast, at the end of tasting hardens slightly.

The best of the best

The monthly magazine "La Bonne Cuisine" organised an interesting blind tasting of twenty-eight brands of Champagne in December 1984. In the presence of Master Chale, Bailiff, this extraordinary contest — a triumph for Michel Budin — pitted the talents of the following tasters against each other: Georges-Albert Aoust, œnologist, founder and director of the Beaune "Wine School"; Philippe Bourguignon, top wine waiter in France and cellar master at Laurent; Christian Mollier, Champagne œnologist, expert for the Reims courts; Philippe Muller, œnologist; Michel Piot, journalist at "Le Figaro"; Philippe Simon, director of "La Bonne Cuisine"; Daniel Willems, barman at the Concorde Lafayette, president of the French barmen's association. Of the twenty-eight tasted, the top five were as follows:

1st: Heidseick Monopole, 6.71 — fine nose, bubbly, long in the mouth, distinct taste;
2nd: Laurent Perrier, 6.64 — elegant, well-structured, pronounced grape, smooth;
3rd: Veuve Clicquot, 6.57 — winey, full Champagne;
4th: Perrier-Jouët, 6.43 — young, lightly dosed Champagne, fine cream, very well done.
5th: Mumm Cordon Rouge, 6.36 — very good Champagne, exotic fruit flavour. A little too much carbon dioxide, average finesse.

Three Champagnes from the Mumm group were classified among the top five. An excellent result which more than pleased the team at Epernay.

Perrier-Jouët 1904

Golden, very fine, long-lasting bubbles. Delicate nose, airy, extremely lacey. A silk veil. Smooth, vanilla flavour. Average length. Colour holds well under oxidation.

Perrier-Jouët 1906

Clear blond to golden a half hour later. Rich nose, honey and grilled almonds, feeling of sweetness in the mouth. Strong, robust, firm with a perfume of vanilla and raisins. Good astringency, but average length.

Perrier-Jouët 1911

A lot of very fine, long-lasting bubbles. Golden, rich nose, intense, concentrated with very ripe fruit: quince, almonds. A wine which seems firm. In the mouth, round, full, harmonious, smooth elegant. Fine flavour. A lot of charm and pleasure. Very long.

Perrier-Jouët 1913

Not much gas. Clear gold. Strong mushroom nose, aeration faded these aromas turning them to humus and woody smells. In the mouth still this flavour of mushrooms with a slight touch of menthol imparting freshness. A little too marked by mushroom to really give pleasure.

Perrier-Jouët 1914

Clear gold, still sparkling. Numerous and long-lasting bubbles. Delicate nose, slight grilled almond aroma. Very great finesse, gives great pleasure. In the mouth still very gassy. Full, velvety, quite a fleshy wine with a feeling of freshness. Toast too. Still a young wine. Very long, splendid. What a future!

Perrier-Jouët 1825: an exceptional bottle

The apotheosis was a truly exceptional Perrier-Jouët of 1825, on the cork "qualité Extra". A Champagne that is one hundred and sixty years old! André Simon and Michael Broadbent class this year as one of the greats for Champagne. A magnificent, hand-blown bottle. The original cork still in place held by a wire clip. The marks made by hemp strings which originally kept it in place are still noticeable on the cork. The bottle is quite full. Monsieur Baveret served it with religious care and for fifteen seconds you could still see some bubbles.

Not as numerous as in the previous series of fine wines that had been tasted but still there. The colour was very pale gold, brilliant. Upon contact with the air it became golden amber coloured, but not at all dark. At the first nose it smelled a bit of reduction but with aeration this ceased. In the aroma could be found baked apples. In the mouth, a round, smooth wine with a lot of fullness; slight taste of toast and grilled almonds. Astonishingly long wine. An exceptional bottle.

I think that I should pay hommage to the person who blended this wine in 1826. One should compare only what is comparable: what wine of the 80's would be compared to this Perrier-Jouët 1825?

What can we learn from this tasting? These are admirable wines that have kept perfectly well. Not one maderized (oxidized), even after having been open for four hours. Over the decades and even for more than a century, they have stayed in the same cold, dark cellar without being touched. These wines must have been very strong Champagnes to start with. Perrier-Jouët have always made it their aim to provide quality, by rigorous selection of grapes and care throughout the entire life of the wine.

Jean-Luc Pouteau: World champion wine waiter.

Champagne and the Belle Epoque
is part of the collection
«Prestige»

This book was written by Nicolas de Rabaudy,
translated by Jill Bennett and David Lord
and edited by la Nouvelle Librairie
43, rue du Chemin Vert
75011 Paris - Tel: 807.24.11

Catalogue number: 288805
Editor's number: 85036
Printed in Spain
I.H.A.S.A., Mallorca, 51, Barcelone
2e semestre 1985
D.L. B-24.733-1985

Photos and illustrations
Cover and page 1: Jacques Kobel (Perrier-Jouët collection); page 2: Lauros-Giraudon (Bibliothèque Nationale); page 4: Roger-Viollet (drawing by M. Carlowski from a photo by M. Neurdein); page 5: Edimédia (drawing by Chéret); pages 6, 8, 10 and 11: J. Kobel (Perrier-Jouët Museum); page 12-49: L. Sully-Jaulmes; pages 14 and 15: Roger Viollet (photos by Boyer); page 16: Lauros-Giraudon (J. Kugel collection); page 19: drawing by Guillaume (Perrier-Jouët collection); page 22: A. Fildier collection; pages 24 and 25: Edimédia (photo by Snark, Kharbine collection); pages 42, 55, 57, 58, 60 and 63: J. Kobel; page 30: Sirot-Ancel collection; page 34: Edimédia (drawing by Cardona); page 37: Roger-Viollet (drawing by Xavier Sager); page 46: Magnum (photo by Burt Glinn); page 50, Perrier-Jouët collection.